JEET KUNE DO
Its Concepts and Philosophies

By Paul Vunak

DEDICATION

I would first and foremost like to dedicate this book to my guru, Dan Inosanto, and secondly, to all of my students who helped make it possible.

ISBN: 0-86568-149-X

Copyright © CFW Enterprises Inc.
All rights reserved.
Printed in the United States of America.

Book Design: Danilo J. Silverio
Edited By: John Corcoran

UNIQUE PUBLICATIONS
4201 Vanowen Place, Burbank, CA 91505

TABLE OF CONTENTS

PREFACE   iv

PART ONE: CONCEPTS   1
    I.   What Color Is Your Belt?   2
    II. First Blood: The Nature of Fighting   6
        A. The Nature of Combat   7
        B. The Four Ranges of Combat   10
        C. Learning Combat Flow   11
        D. The Twenty-Six Fighting Elements of Jun-Fan   13
    III. The Role of Kali   14
    IV. Filling the Cup: The Art of Change   17

PART TWO: ATTRIBUTES   23
    V.   The Point of No Return: Instinct to Kill   24
        A. JKD's Mental Principles of Combat   25
        B. Using Killer Instinct   27
        C. The Causes of Fear   28
        D. Beyond the Fear of Death   29
    VI. Are You Grounded?   31
        A. Footwork   31
        B. Coordination   32
        C. Line Familiarization   34
    VII. The Broken Blur   36
        A. Speed   36
        B. Broken Rhythm   39
    VIII. Awareness   41
        A. Kinesthetic Perception   41
        B. Where to Stare   42
        C. The Peripheral Opponent   43
    IX. NOT-Kune Do   46
        A. Simply Eclectic   46
        B. No Room for Politics   47
        C. Complacency   49
        D. Streetfighting...Not Even Comparable!!   50
    X.   A Parting Shot   52

PART THREE: APPLICATIONS   55

ABOUT THE AUTHOR   123

PREFACE

Before you read this book, there are two things that I must have you understand from the beginning. They are essential, and yet, when you first read them you'll probably be scratching your head.

First, Jeet Kune Do does not exist! And second, you can't learn a martial art from a book. Just as you can't learn the piano, or a foreign language, by reading a book. Here's why.

Jeet Kune Do (JKD) is, to many, a mystical, intangible thing that everyone wants but nobody seems to be able to find. Students come from hundreds of miles, like zealous disciples, to attend a JKD seminar...for a paltry eight hours. Many, learned in other art forms, have heard of this maniacal, combative, deadly study, but cannot find where it is taught, who teaches it, and what is really different about it.

The problem is not one of shrouds of mystery so much as it is a sheer lack of human beings — human beings who *really know* how to teach JKD concepts. Notice that I say concepts, and not Jeet Kune Do. That is because JKD exists only as you exist. If you feel a certain way, it changes a certain way. If you don't nurture it, it becomes lazy within you. If you polish and hone it, it changes into your opponent's worst nightmare. It is *you* that gives JKD it's existence. One of my students gave me a small placard that reads:

> "Jeet Kune Do, ultimately, is not a matter of petty technique. It is not a question of developing what has already been developed, but of recovering what has been left behind. These things [JKD concepts] have always been with us...*in us...all the time.* And have never been lost or distorted except by our misguided manipulation of them."
>
> – BRUCE LEE

To make it simple, Bruce simply meant that he discovered—while going through the rigors of establishing a fighting method with his best friend, Dan Inosanto—that what he came up with was a martial art that exists in all of us. We already know JKD. That is why it is so easy to learn, and why it seems always to be so aptly tailored to each individual.

That is also why you won't be able to find your own JKD from a book. *You* don't exist in here. These are my words, my teaching techniques, my "way" to do it. Pure JKD involves taking what is useful (including what you read here) and discarding what is useless (including what you read here). Woven throughout this book is the use of the term "flight time." That is a key. An F-15 pilot cannot learn to maneuver an Eagle from a book. Books can help, but he must first learn the basics of flying, then graduate up until his own hindquarters are strapped into that seat. Pulling a seven-G turn just can't be described in the written word. Neither can experiencing a *jik jun choy*, or "straight-blast," in JKD. You have to experience it!

Why, then, a book? An instruction manual? Everything from your vacuum cleaner to that F-15 has one...and filling your mind with important facts, data, and other situational and training information is essential. It helps to fill in a hole. I will try to make sense of what JKD is to me, what it can be to you, and how its principles can be applied not only in a combative situation, but in the everyday rigors of life itself. Stay with me.

Paul Vunak
Los Angeles, California

PART ONE:
CONCEPTS

CHAPTER I
WHAT COLOR IS YOUR BELT?

It is a familiar and tragi-comedic tale, and you'll hear it repeated numerous times throughout this book. A black belt with years of training is easily beaten in a *real fight* by an unschooled street kid. The black belt's years of rigorous training were of no avail. Why?

The outcome in such incidents is not determined by the respective fighter's technical expertise, but by his respective *attributes*. Attributes are the inner qualities that shape technique...that provide the ground from which technique springs. The victor in a fight is the fighter who possesses superior attributes. These include the qualities of killer instinct, sensitivity, timing, reflex, power, line familiarization, sense of purpose, and yes, technical skill.

Consider sports. There are always individuals who dominate their game. They do so *not* because they know the techniques of the game, but because they possess superior attributes. For instance, millions can play basketball, countless thousands can dribble, pass and shoot with great skill. But how many of those countless thousands possess the attributes that elevate a player like Larry Bird to the realm of basketball legend. In football, how many players possess the attributes of an Eric Dickerson or a Walter Payton?

As it is in sport, so it is in martial arts. It is not technique, but the refinement of attributes that accounts for the superior fighter. As I have said before, *attributes* are the primary focus of Jeet Kune Do training. Those who try to label or classify JKD through cataloging its technical repertoire are misguided. (Remember...it doesn't exist.) Jeet Kune Do is not

Paul demonstrating a takedown.

about techniques or movements in and of themselves. JKD is concerned with the manner in which techniques and movements are performed.

What is a Jeet Kune Do technique? It is the jab that is felt before it is seen; it is the jab that causes terrible damage; it is the jab thrown at the perfect moment in a fight; it is the jab that is not telegraphed to the opponent. A jab that does not possess those qualities — those attributes — is merely a jab, *not* a Jeet Kune Do technique.

JKD is an iceberg. The tip is technique, while lurking below the surface is the great mass of the berg, which is composed of attributes. And as an experienced seaman well knows, it is the hidden mass of an iceberg that constitutes the greatest danger.

To give one example of the nature of JKD training as it relates to developing attributes, let's consider the Kali stick. Introduced as a training device by Dan Inosanto, the Kali stick is from the Filipino martial arts, which have been woven into the framework of JKD. Consider the single stick, and how it develops a key attribute — that of reflex. Wielded by a trained man, the single stick has been clocked traveling at speeds of up to 150 m.p.h. By way of reference, Goose Gossage's fastball travels at a relatively slow 95 m.p.h.

The experience of full-contact sparring with the stick (and *lots* of protective equipment) over an extended period of time forces your neurological centers to operate at a much higher level. In short, your reflexes get a helluva lot faster. This becomes apparent when one makes the transition to empty-hand sparring. The fastest punch moves in slow motion. This is like the sensation of slowness that you experience when driving 55 m.p.h. after driving at consistently higher speeds...such as 95! Fifty-five may be fast, but the previous experience of 95 m.p.h. makes it seem *very* slow.

Another important attribute in JKD is sensitivity. Sensitivity allows one to quickly and accurately *feel*, not see, what the opponent is doing in order to react in the most efficient manner. Again, to practice this attribute JKD uses knife sparring, to increase the speed and sensitivity. When you spar with wooden knives, they are treated as real, and any contact with the body is considered critical, if not sufficient to end the engagement. This being so, the degree of sensitivity called for in such close-quarters sparring is particularly high. There is no margin for error. When one then returns to empty-hand fighting, where solid hits and not mere touches matter, the student discovers that his sensitivity has quadrupled.

As these examples indicate, attributes in Jeet Kune Do are far more important than techniques, which explains why it is hard to define JKD to someone used to distinguishing arts *by* their techniques. The difficulty in getting this point across is compounded by the tremendous variety of techniques in JKD. Indeed, all of the techniques of Jeet Kune Do ever published comprise only two percent of the techniques actually used. In order to understand and internalize JKD principles, it is necessary to have a different mentality — *you* are Jeet Kune Do!

CHAPTER II
FIRST BLOOD: THE NATURE OF FIGHTING

Present day misconceptions about Jeet Kune Do are legion: "JKD doesn't really exist" [like I said earlier]; "It died with Bruce Lee"; "JKD is a composition of styles"; "JKD is anything that works" ; "Bruce Lee created a style that only he could do" ; "JKD is a modified form of Wing Chun"; etc., etc.

This confusion about Jeet Kune Do is entirely understandable. Its charismatic founder lived a brief, spectacular life that ended suddenly and mysteriously. His most important work, *The Tao of Jeet Kune Do,* is a collection of unpolished notes published after his death. For several reasons, including the insistence of many on viewing JKD as what Bruce Lee portrayed on screen, his top disciples have been reluctant to publicize the art.

Another reason adding to this confusion is that the art is hard to define within the framework of linear logic that most Western people prefer. This linear logic defines various martial arts by variations in their techniques: where the knee is located during a side kick; the formation of the fist in a hand technique (reverse punch, for example, or crane beak, tiger claw, leopard paw, etc.); the nature of a style's movement, be it linear or circular; the type of stances used.

In contrast, Jeet Kune Do defines itself as "using no way as way, no limitation as limitation." For many, particularly those burned in the past by martial arts "mumbo-jumbo," such a statement is difficult to grasp. I have thus far outlined the pivotal role that personal attributes and their development play in JKD. Now I would like to turn to the other half of the art — how JKD uses those attributes in combat.

It is not an accident that throughout this book you will re-read the example of a black belt losing to a streetfighter, or a more inexperienced fighter. JKD is *not* a tournament or a ring sport! Its sole purpose is to develop efficiency in fighting. Efficiency not only in one-on-one, empty-hand encounters, but also in confrontations involving weapons or multiple opponents. One thus needs to discuss the nature of fighting.

The Nature of Combat

A JKD man or woman does not concern him or herself with meeting the average streetfighter or "black belt." Rather, one pictures fighting a crazed Lyle Alzado high on PCP. When one can vividly picture that spectacle, one realizes that *a streetfight takes place in all four combat ranges.* This image also provides a dose of reality and a movement away from the mentality fostered by the "Billy Jack-type" films. As Bruce Lee observed, "A fight is not usually won by one punch or kick; you must learn to endure…or hire yourself a bodyguard and lead a less aggressive life."

It was with that thought in mind that Lee turned to the formulation of JKD. Between 1964 and 1973, Lee, with the assistance of Dan Inosanto, dissected every fighting art that the two could discover. Out of several hundred systems, Lee selected elements from 26 styles to form the foundation of Jeet Kune Do. On the average, five-to-ten percent of any of the 26 arts was utilized in JKD; in certain cases, just training methods or combat theory was used. (As in the case of Western fencing, which lent its concept of the "stop-hit," a simultaneous parry and counter, to JKD's combat philosophy…and, indeed, to JKD's very name.)

Many sincere martial artists attempt, on their own, what they think Bruce Lee did — study several styles and pick and choose favorite techniques from each. Although their im-

Paul Vunak is the hand-to-hand instructor for the U.S. Navy Special Warfare Department. He is shown here with one of the teams in Virginia Beach, Virginia.

pulse might be the same (meaning, an understanding of the incompleteness of most styles), this is not Jeet Kune Do, nor Bruce Lee's approach.

Guided by principles of attributes and the realities of combat, JKD requires the instantaneous transition from art to art while fighting. To allow for this the elements of the chosen arts must fit harmoniously together.

To use a simple example, Shotokan Karate's chambered fist position (hand on hip) cannot move into Wing Chun trapping techniques with the necessary economy of motion. One does not move arbitrarily from art to art. Rather, one responds with the most efficient attribute (or art) to the ever-changing energy, movement, and range of the opponent(s). This is what Lee meant in the statement, "My movement is a result of your movement, my technique is a result of your technique." To understand how the elements of the selected 26 arts are put together in JKD, one must turn to the concept of *range*.

The Four Ranges of Combat

Regardless of style, there are four combat ranges: kicking range, punching range, trapping range, and grappling range. Most martial artists spend their lives learning techniques that fit one, or sometimes two of these ranges, depending on their art. Regardless of their range of specialization, most martial artists assume they can fight, and finish, an encounter at *their* chosen range. Given the image already mentioned, of confronting Lyle Alzado on PCP, such an assumption is dangerous. Such an assumption can prove fatal.

A few examples illustrate that point. A Tae Kwon Do student is usually taught that legs are stronger than arms. An opponent won't get past his kicks. Thus, the art teaches some punching techniques, but heavily emphasizes kicking. When students spar, they usually start out at a long — or kicking — range, throwing bombs at one another. Rarely do they attempt to close the gap, and if they do, they virtually *never* remain at close range for long. The effect of this type of training is that the student never tests the premise that he can keep the fight at kicking range. What happens to him when the opponent moves in during a real encounter?

This criticism is not limited to styles that stress long-range fighting. Wing Chun is an excellent art in the trapping range. On the other hand, if a wrestler were to get the Wing Chun man on the ground, the Wing Chun practitioner is out of his natural environment and at a great disadvantage. Grappling is a common tactic of large and strong attackers. Yet grappling and locking arts, such as Jujutsu and Aikido, are usually based on the assumption that the opponent grabs you first. There are very few Jujutsu schools that kick, box, and then trap to enter into locking/grappling range to apply their specialty techniques. The essential point here is that *there is no superior art!*

All systems of martial art have their strong points and weak points. Bruce Lee observed, "There is a range in which Western boxing will counter any kicking art. There is a range in which Wing Chun will counter boxing. There is a range where Tai Chi Chuan will counter Wing Chun." In short, Lee selected elements of 26 different arts to give his students an integrated framework that prepared them to fight any opponent at any range.

Those who witnessed Lee at any of his closed-door sparring sessions saw this principle in action. Limited by the vocabulary of their time, these witnesses were never able to find a label for Lee. One moment, he would dance and shuffle at long range…boxing with his lead foot, hitting the opponent at heretofore unknown angles like an experienced Savate man. If the opponent countered, Lee would bob and weave and throw body shots like a professional boxer. Upon being blocked by the opponent, he would shift into Wing Chun's *jik chun choy* ("straight blast"), trapping any obstruction, pummeling with a flurry of fists and elbows, and ending the encounter with a Jujustu-like flip. All of these difficult elements would appear in a "match" that lasted just ten seconds!

Learning Combat Flow

Learning to be like Bruce Lee, flowing responsively from one martial art to another in an engagement, sounds a lot simpler than it really is. The trainee must first accomplish two things simultaneously: the elements from the 26 styles must be learned, and one's personal attributes must be developed to their fullest. Regarding attributes, consider a basketball player by way of example. He might be able to do all the movements required to perform a slam dunk, but *those* attributes are useless because he lacks one essential quality — the leg strength to propel him above the rim.

Once the student has progressed sufficiently on these two fronts, he moves into a third stage with training drills such as *hu-bud* (Kali energy-exchanging drills) and *chi sao* (Wing Chun's "sticking hands" exercise) practice. JKD's *chi sao* differs from its Wing Chun counterpart in that JKD practitioners are not limited to executing Wing Chun techniques only. Any technique from the 26 core arts is allowed. The game of *chi sao* is very different when one or the other partner can use arm or nerve destructions (drawn from Kali), throws, or any other JKD technique. Once the student is able to flow throughout the 26 arts during JKD drills, he is ready for the fourth stage of JKD development, sparring.

In sparring, it is imperative that the instructor oversee and regulate the intensity of the match. Egos can flare easily. Students need to be shown how to work *with* each other to create the most conducive environment for flowing through and changing arts in midstream. Once many hours of this type of sparring "flight time" has been logged, the instructor can gradually increase the tempo of the sparring until the students are engaging in full contact with protective equipment.

The end result of JKD training is the production of a man who possesses no structure or form. Hence, he possesses *all* structures, *all* forms. He is able to adapt to any situation, like water adjusting to the shape of any container. Able, for example, to fill an empty cup.

THE TWENTY-SIX FIGHTING ELEMENTS OF JUN FAN

1. Wing Chun
2. Northern Praying Mantis
3. Southern Praying Mantis
4. Choy Li Fut
5. Tai-Chi Chuan (Wu Family style)
6. Paqua
7. Hsing-I
8. Bak-Hoo Pai (White Crane)
   Bak-Fu Pai (White Tiger)
9. Eagle Claw
10. Ng Ga Kuen (Five Family System)
11. Ny Ying Ga (Five Animal System)
12. Bak Mei Pai (White Eyebrow)
13. Northern Shaolin
14. Southern Shaolin
15. Bok Pai
16. Law Horn Kuen
17. Chin Na
18. Monkey Style
19. Drunken Style
20. Western Fencing (Foil)
21. Western Boxing
22. Western Wrestling
23. Jujustu
24. Escrima
25. Filipino Sikaran
26. Muay Thai (Thai Boxing)

CHAPTER III
THE ROLE OF KALI

Recently there has been a surge of conjecture regarding the evolution of Jeet Kune Do. I do not intend to define JKD here, as that is explored in greater depth elsewhere, but rather to clarify an absurd misconception regarding Kali's role in JKD's evolution.

Bruce Lee's original art was Wing Chun. After seeing certain limitations in Wing Chun (or any *one* art), the next obvious step was to investigate the principles, concepts, and techniques of various arts. The process of this investigation is the very essence of JKD.

In 1964, Dan Inosanto first met Bruce Lee. At that time, Mr. Inosanto already held black belts in several other arts, and was a world-class martial artist in his own right. Dan's athletic ability was, and is, at an uncommon level. At 145 pounds, and standing 5'6," Dan was the leading ground-gainer at Wentworth College, running the 100-yard dash in near world-record time, 9.4 seconds. These points all became moot after sparring with Bruce for just a few seconds!

Immediately after this first encounter, Dan became Bruce Lee's student. Over the next nine years, both Bruce and Dan literally dissected and synthesized every martial art and philosophy salient to the concept of JKD, streetfighting! They absorbed what was useful, rejected what was useless, and added what was specifically their own. Over the next nine-year period, Dan Inosanto remained, with Bruce, the integral catalyst behind the mutual development of the style/concept that is now known as Jeet Kune Do. This procedure began by blending popular arts like Western boxing to the more sublime, less-known styles such as Drunken Monkey, Chin

From left to right: Bill "Superfoot" Wallace, Daniel Duby and the author.

Na, and Bak Mei Pai. There were approximately 26 different styles which lent themselves to the overall synthesis of JKD.

Of the many highly-skilled students that Bruce Lee taught during his lifetime, only three ever qualified to teach Jeet Kune Do — James Lee (deceased), Ted Wong, and Dan Inosanto. The unspoken and intrinsic credential for Dan Inosanto is embodied in the fact that, after Bruce's departure into film, he was conferred the responsibility of maintaining the true authenticity of JKD.

After Bruce Lee's death in 1973, Mr. Inosanto, Bruce's protege, continued to cultivate and refine the original process by which he and Bruce developed Jeet Kune Do. This process is not static; it is dynamic in nature and continues to evolve, as was Bruce's intention. Dan's contribution greatly improved JKD's efficiency. This fact is agreed upon by anyone who takes the time to *objectively* compare the differences.

There are some who have insinuated otherwise, stating that Kali has diluted JKD. The notion that Dan's integration of Kali (the 27th art) in any way, shape, or form is diluting the essence of JKD is absurd! Could anyone be so naive in their thinking to assume that the addition of another aspect of a functional art makes JKD any less effective? Did art number 13 dilute art number 12? Did art number 25 dilute art number 24? The answer is obvious.

CHAPTER IV
FILLING THE CUP: THE ART OF CHANGE

I would like to address one of the core themes behind Jeet Kune Do, the ability to continuously change and adapt. This book is entitled *The Empty Cup* because of Bruce Lee's statement that we always should retain learning like a cup — never allowing it to become full, always allowing it to be absorbed or emptied, so that one's learning process might not be hindered. Also, he said that we should become like water, able to reshape ourselves continuously, taking on the form of our container – more analogies to adaptation and change.

The cup should always be refilled after the knowledge held therein is absorbed into the system. This requires the flow of continuous change and adaptation. Martial arts are an expression of the self; so, too, is anything one does in life. Yet fighting, and it's study, are different from most other things. They involve the physical well-being of the self. And one's manner of self-preservation is a direct statement of that person's individual psyche.

Just as a psychologist learns about the inner personality of his patients through listening, a wise martial arts instructor learns about the inner personality of his students by observing. People express themselves emotionally and mentally through the way they move physically.

Without ever watching Bruce Lee throw one kick or punch, people who met him agreed that perhaps he was one of the

The author (right) with his Savate instructor, Daniel Duby. The two opened the first Savate school in the United States, in Redondo Beach, California, in 1980.

most intense individuals they had ever met. It was no coincidence that this intensity manifested itself physically when he moved.

Just as one's physical movement reveals one's emotional makeup, the structure of one's martial art reveals the structure of one's mentality. The structure of JKD, the art that Bruce Lee founded, has no one structure — the point being to adapt *from* structure to structure, and ultimately develop complete spontaneity free from all structures. If one can flow from structure to structure physically, one is more likely to achieve in life the ultimate goal of so many spiritual thinkers: continuous change and adaptation. As Carlos Casteneda's Don Juan says, "A warrior must be perennially fluid and shift harmoniously with the world around him." Lao Tsu had the same idea with his notion of water conforming to all structures. Even Western science, in books such as *The Global Brain* by Peter Russell, has arrived at the same place. For Russell, life itself can be defined as a means to "take in, process, and cast out matter and energy and [to] have detectable effects upon [the] physical surroundings." Thus, if there is life, there is continuous change in the physical surroundings and, therefore, if one's own life is to continue, one must change too.

As Bruce Lee's book, *The Tao of Jeet Kune Do*, shows, Bruce had absorbed the concept of continuous change and adaptation, which happens to be the very essence of Jeet Kune Do. Jeet Kune Do is not a tournament-oriented art. It is, on a physical level, about streetfighting. Although combative sports such as boxing, wrestling, and kickboxing can be found in JKD, they are present only for the purpose of developing attributes necessary for fighting.

Again, the concept of attributes — speed, timing, coordination, strength, balance, flexibility, toughness, footwork, etc. — is *central* to Jeet Kune Do. It is these qualities, of which technique is included, that determines who wins a fight. By definition, a fight is won by the man who has a superior mix of attributes. In Jeet Kune Do, the trick is to use the attributes appropriately.

Just as you wouldn't teach people to swim by throwing them into deep water, or to ski by taking them to the top of a mountain, or to learn surgery by giving them patients, so, too, should you not teach people to fight by throwing them into fights. They must first be prepared. And how does one "prepare" attributes? One of the most important attributes (of which we will dedicate an entire chapter) is called "killer instinct." This happens to be the "fight" half of the flight or fight syndrome — an adrenaline rush. To use it with maximum efficacy, one must be able to turn it on and off, perhaps several times, within a fight.

Fighting from outside range (the concept of range being another topic of discussion) — i.e., kicking and boxing range — calls for being light on the feet, sticking and moving, slipping, and most importantly, "stop hitting." To be able to perform these maneuvers, you need attributes such as line familiarization, balance, agility, coordination, awareness, and a cool, detached intensity. In many respects, this is the antithesis of what happens during the adrenaline rush.

When the fight or flight syndrome occurs, the hypothalamus and pituitary glands send an impulse to the adrenal gland, which in turn secretes adrenaline instantly to the body, producing a "turbo-charge" emotionally, mentally, and physically. The attributes that JKD uses which are most affected by this turbo blast are those needed in close-range fighting, such as aggressiveness, strength, and pain tolerance. The attributes that are decreased are those cited earlier for fighting at longer ranges. Thus, as a fight changes ranges, one must be able to constantly change and adapt by turning the adrenaline rush/killer instinct on and off, and vice-versa. Only a person of well-above-average clarity can easily and responsibly do both.

Just as we continuously change and adapt killer instinct and other attributes, we must continually change and adapt structures in order to respect the concepts of "economy of motion" and responsiveness. By "structures," we are actually talking about martial styles. Bruce Lee once said," There's a range in which Western boxing will counter any kicking art. There is a range where Tai Chi Chuan will counter Wing Chun." In other words, *if no structure is superior all the time, one must choose the structure that is superior at the moment.*

This does not mean that you need to learn every martial art. Once again, what Bruce Lee did, with Dan Inosanto's help, was to analyze every fighting system he could. Out of hundreds of systems analyzed, Lee chose "elements" from 26 arts. Naturally, these elements were not only the combative, but were designed to fit together in a way that allows for continuous change and adaptation in a fight.

Lurking beneath the surface of this approach is the fact that each structure has a "mentality." Savate is continuous movement and pinpoint finesse; Thai boxing is ruggedness and power; Wing Chun is directness and aggressiveness; Tai-

Chi is harmonious use of the opponent's energy, etc. In other words, continuous change and adaptation from structure to structure require the ability to change and adapt mentalities.

For example, you could be picking apart an opponent from long range with boxing and Savate, and your opponent, a large man bent on your destruction, suddenly rushes in like a wild man, closing the gap. Having another structure and mentality at your quick disposal allows you to avoid meeting his superior force head-on, and instead shift into a Tai-Chi defense, diverting his energy and setting him up for a barrage of elbows, knees and head-butts from the Filipino art of Kali. Thus, in a matter of seconds, you have gone from Savate and boxing to Tai-Chi and Kali.

This martial arts evolution starts on a physical level and progresses to an emotional/mental level. The next step toward the spiritual door is to apply the ability to adapt and change in everyday life. Though touched upon in this chapter, we shall delve further into the "spiritual" side of Jeet Kune Do, and truly find out how it is not unlike thread that interweaves itself, if practiced correctly, through our lives.

PART TWO:
ATTRIBUTES

CHAPTER FIVE
THE POINT OF NO RETURN: INSTINCT TO KILL

One of the highest stages of martial arts lies beyond the mere realm of technique. While many martial artists feel that technical mastery of their style entitles them to be called "masters," the truth is that technique is *not an end*, but rather a means to an end. The goal of martial arts is mastery of the mind. The training methods and techniques used are merely tools, and the relative merit of each tool consists of its amenability in developing the practitioner's personal attributes and bringing him or her to mastery of the mind. Moreover, ninety percent of the outcome of a battle is determined by the respective mental states of the combatants. This is because the mind is the strongest weapon in the fighter's arsenal.

For most people, the mind consists only of "scattered energy." Those who achieve greatness, in whatever endeavor, are those who can harness and focus that energy. We all know stories that illustrate the power of the mind. The physically frail mother who defends her children with superhuman strength; the person who jumps from a burning building at a height which would break his legs on any other occasion, but who does so unharmed. Because the mind is the ultimate source of power, it is not surprising that all advanced arts, regardless of their apparent dissimilarities, turn out, upon close observation, to be based on principles and concepts that are virtually *interchangeable*!

At a seminar at the California Martial Arts Academy. From left to right: Hawkins Cheung, the author, Jessie Glover, William Cheung, Dan Inosanto, Tim Tackett and Ted Lucaylucay.

The evolution of Jeet Kune Do, especially under Dan Inosanto, is a perfect example of this fact. With true insight, Inosanto perceived that the JKD he learned from Bruce Lee during their long and close association was based upon the same principles as his own art of Kali. Therefore, the JKD currently taught freely *blends* the two arts. Because JKD stresses that the student must "absorb what is useful," and since Kali, through centuries of rigorous testing in combat, has evolved to a very high level, there is no barrier presented by a "traditionalist" mentality to prevent one from freely integrating Kali with Jeet Kune Do.

JKD's Mental Principles of Combat

What then, are the principles concerning the all important mental state for fighting as taught by Jeet Kune Do? To answer this question, we need to reemphasize the idea of the JKD man's manner of fighting. When he is out of kicking range, he remains calm in order to be able to anticipate the opponent's moves with awareness, using the correct counters, or "stop hits," that are dictated by the situation while still moving in such a way as to be able to "pot shot" his opponent — closing the gap for his rapid striking, blasting and trapping techniques. This particular stage of a fight in JKD is called the "rally." This is the time to "turn it on" with all of the killer instinct possible. If for some reason the rally were to fail, and the gap opened again, the JKD man must be able to click his killer instinct on and off again at will, according to the range that he is in.

Although there is a clear distinction between theatrical and functional JKD, Bruce Lee, in his movies, showed very clearly what is meant here. In outside range, he was relaxed but ready, cat-like, dancing, wearing his famous sardonic smile or a look of bored contempt on his face. However, as he closed the gap, he became a banshee of frightening and intimidating intensity. The killer instinct showed clearly and totally, yet the instant the range opened again, he instantly reverted to a state of cool calm.

Killer instinct goes by many names: guts, meanness, craziness, going ape-shit, psycho, etc. Whatever this aggressive mental state is called, it is the essential ingredient to being able to fight well. What few people realize is that *everyone in the world has killer instinct and is capable of possessing it to the same degree.*

The difference between Saddam Hussein and Tim Conway is nothing more than the threshold at which this quality — this killer instinct — erupts. Each person's threshold is different. For one, all it takes is someone cutting him off in traffic. For another, it would take a situation highly charged with danger to himself or loved ones. The reasons for differences in individual thresholds is not always clear, but they seem related to factors of conditioning, upbringing, environment, heredity, and, most of all, decisions made by the individual, either consciously or subconsciously.

An aware instructor helps guide the student to conscious knowledge of his threshold. The insights which accompany the student's new understanding of himself in this respect are powerful tools in the process of mastering the mind. Having achieved this self-knowledge, the student may choose to increase or lower his threshold with his instructor's assistance.

Using Killer Instinct

Since killer instinct is present in every one of us, the question becomes what to do with it. Some believe that it is better to ignore it, to pretend that it doesn't exist. Others acknowledge its existence and declare it evil or, at the very least, a mental state to be rigorously suppressed. But I believe that those individuals who have not come to terms with this side of themselves harbor a deep intranquility, whether they hide it well or not.

For example, when such an individual is confronted by a situation in which maturity dictates that there *is* no real need to fight, he will do the right thing — and not fight — but feel disgusted and contemptuous of himself. Why? Although perhaps only unconsciously, it is because he is aware that he has not come to grips with his killer instinct and knows that had he been required to fight, he would have been a coward.

In contrast, a person who knows how to tap into his killer instinct also does the "right thing," but continues to feel at ease with himself. The wise martial artist cultivates the seed of killer instinct within his or her being, and trims and controls it. It can serve him.

The key is to control killer instinct to the degree that it can be turned on and off at will. The ability to do so requires, first, that one knows himself, and second, that one has self-confidence. Killer instinct is dependent upon self-respect and self-confidence. In order to attain self-confidence, the first step is to master technique. Obviously, if one does not know how to fight, one is not going to be confident. No confidence, no killer instinct.

At the same time that the student is perfecting his techniques, he must develop the discipline of self examination, ruthlessly rooting out negative thoughts from the mind.

The mind creates what it believes. For example, one of the most common mistakes made in an encounter is predetermining the outcome by judging the opponent. Thinking, "I would sure hate to mess with him," or, "Look at the size of his neck!" This kind of input is exceedingly detrimental to one's ability to fight at that very moment. The second that the opponent intimidates one in some way, killer instinct flies out the window. The same is true in strange situations where one is intimidated in another way. *The worst enemy of a fight is fear, so analyze what causes intimidation, and why. Then take corrective action.*

The Causes of Fear

If you fear closing the gap and fighting in close, it's probably because you're not good at it. The solution is easy enough; take the time to improve your infighting. Do *not* kid yourself with bland assertions about the leg being longer and stronger than the arm, and therefore kicking is best.

If you fear forgetting your art in the moment of crisis, you are probably right; you're training method may be incomplete. In many styles other than JKD, it is customary to defend against angles of attack only within the confines of the schools, or art's, style. Obviously, in the street you will probably run into something different and be in trouble, because you have developed the attribute of line familiarization (which will be discussed later). You are surprised by something you haven't seen before.

When I studied Tae Kwon Do, for example, I was defending against roundhouse kicks and side kicks. When I studied Hung Gar, I was blocking crane beak and claw attacks, and in Kenpo, it was reverse punches and backfists. The solution is a realistic training regimen that includes sparring under *all* conditions and locations, full-contact training (with proper gear), loud, abusive emotional training, and so forth. With this type of training, you can adapt to whatever situation arises.

At the same time you are training to remove the fears which hinder you, you do *not* want to — nor, in all likelihood, *can* you — eliminate their handmaiden, the adrenaline rush. In training you have to simulate the stimuli of an actual encounter as closely as possible. Remember a frightening feeling from the past to trigger the same rushes of adrenaline — anger, fear, anxiety, and butterflies — that you felt *then* while you are training *now!* Make the imagination a powerful tool.

Beyond the Fear of Death

Once a martial artist has achieved a realistic level of proficiency in technique, self-knowledge, confidence, and the attendant ability to tap into his killer instinct, he can presumably deal with almost any situation which arises. However, two types of situations require even more from the martial arts.

In one type of situation, a fair assessment shows that success is only a possibility, not a probability. Here, the student must be clear enough in his thoughts to realize that the best thing that he can do, is to act as if he believed in victory, thus maintaining his killer instinct.

The other type of situation is perhaps the hardest. It is where defeat and even death appear inevitable. What an individual does when faced with overwhelming odds reveals much, if not all, about his inner character, clarity of purpose, and belief system — or lack thereof. The Filipinos developed an interesting belief system which enables them to deal with all types of situations, including the ones just discussed. They believe that the outcome of any encounter has already been determined by a Higher Being, so they go in with the attitude of going all out. Since the outcome has already been chosen, they have no psychic hindrances preventing them from giving their all.

Bruce Lee said, "You must be like a rag doll. No fear. No anxiety. No doubt can enter your mind. There is no time to regret once a fight has started. You cannot change your mind or question yourself in the face of action. Do not be concerned with escaping safely! Let him smash your flesh, and you fracture his bone. Let him fracture your bone, and you take his life. Lay your life before him."

When the mind is so at peace that it can calmly function in the face of death, then we can say that the individual has achieved mastery of the self and inner-peace. By this criterion, the Filipino tradition has been very successful in producing fine masters. It is no accident that virtually all of them were deeply religious. Their inner blades were very sharp indeed!

The ability to use killer instinct when appropriate is essential and a slippery stepping stone to finally being at peace with yourself. Even Ghandi felt that violence was preferable to cowardice. Only when fear (of the sort that causes cowardice) has been overcome, can man honestly contemplate pacifism without running the risk of self-patronization with endless rationalization.

In short, we have discussed that one of the highest goals of martial arts is the mastery of the mind to achieve inner-peace; how the mental dimension is ultimately the most important dimension in fighting; the long and close range mental states of the JKD fighter, and the crucial element of killer instinct, and how one achieves it. It is achieved through a process of developing self-awareness, technical proficiency, confidence, the elimination of fear as a negative input, and familiarity with the adrenaline rush. We also discussed why this killer instinct should be developed and not ignored or repressed. The last point dealt with clarity of purpose and the belief systems necessary when facing the possibility of inevitable defeat.

Remember that to everything, there is its opposite. To understand what is polite, you must first experience rudeness. In order to be at peace within yourself, you must first be in touch with your killer instinct. To *be* at peace, you must be able to be violent. There is no front without a back.

CHAPTER VI
ARE YOU GROUNDED?

Footwork

"Footwork is probably one of the most important qualities a fighter can possess," says Dan Inosanto. The ability to put your body where you want it in relation to one's opponent dictates the outcome of *every* movement launched during the fight (both offensively and defensively). The problem with most martial artists stems from their mentality. Most martial artists believe that they can concoct some stance that will "hide" their vital organs, and their likelihood of being injured will be reduced. This either puts them in some sort of convoluted, static posture (which is imitating either some animal or insect, with which our morphology has nothing to do!), or in their quest for stability instead of mobility their legs end up so wide and their bodies so low, that they would have difficulty getting out of the way of a cartwheel, much less a fast jab.

In Bruce Lee's quest for street reality, he and Dan Inosanto came upon certain truths. "In long range, where punches and kicks are being thrown, one does not need stability (unless you're in a push-fight), one needs *agility* to evade punches, while still being able to counterpunch, kick and stop-hit without telegraphing." This truth led them to arts such as Western boxing, Kali, fencing, Savate, etc. — all in which the common denominator is movement, fakes, broken rhythm, and so on. As these truths were developed, certain individuals were hand-picked who possessed these qualities at an uncommon level. Bruce would spend hours watching tapes of Muhammad Ali, or Sugar Ray Robinson. Dan Inosanto

Dan Inosanto (right) and Paul at an Aspen seminar in 1980.

spent years studying every nuance of John LaCoste, one of his many Kali instructors. "To this day," Dan says, "my footwork doesn't compare to John LaCoste's in his late eighties!"

If Bruce were alive now, he would certainly marvel at Sugar Ray Leonard, who I believe, in his time, has perhaps the best footwork in the business. If Leonard would pursue his footwork outside the realm of boxing, I believe he would see himself at an embryonic stage, compared to his potential in his fifties or sixties. The legs go out first in boxers due to the nature of the game. Since endurance is probably a more viable attribute than most, boxers tend to be like drag-strip cars that go for the short run and burn out quicker, as opposed to a Rolls Royce that, if treated with care, appreciates over the years.

Coordination

Remember during your high school days, while playing sports, one guy always seemed to "cruise along," doing

Dan Inosanto and Paul conducting a seminar in Aspen, Colorado in 1981.

everything right. In basketball, he was usually the playmaker, in football the quarterback, and in baseball probably the pitcher. While everyone else worked hard, and still made natural mistakes, this guy hardly came to practice and never made mistakes. Some players could be observed, and it was quite obvious why they excelled: their size, their strength, leaping ability, etc. This "other" guy had just an average build. There was nothing you could put your finger on to determine why he was so good. He was just *good. Real good.*

The attribute that he possessed to a very high level was coordination. The word coordination literally means "the harmonious functioning of interrelated muscles, organs, bones, and nerves." Coordination comes naturally to some people, and it can be *taught* to all people. This is why Dan Inosanto, myself, and a few others have been telling people for years to work weapons.

The level of coordination that it takes to work sticks, knives, staffs, double sticks, and so on. is five times greater than anything empty hand. Since coordination is universal, when we *return* back to empty hands, we are five times more coordinated. Now let's talk about what effect coordination has directly on martial arts.

Well, through the eyes of a JKD man, I can tell you that coordination, on a rudimentary level, helps literally everything we do. On a more functional level, it gives one the ability to apply much, much more pressure on the opponent. (Due to the fact that this person is being assaulted from both hands and feet, elbows, knees, head-butts, eye-jabs, arm wrenches, and nerve destructions.) All of these weapons are *coordinated* to a micro-second. Now the practitioner can free the mind from the thought process, and let the all-important attribute — coordination — take over.

Here are some major ways you can improve *your* coordination. Implement weapons training in your curriculum. Rhythm and coordination go hand in hand. Start fiddling around with bongos or drums. Learn to use both hands and feet simultaneously.

All sports require a degree of coordination, however, some more than others. Here are some suggestions. Handball, basketball, tennis. Perform any desired movement *blindfolded*. This increases the visualization process and the necessity for coordination.

Line Familiarization

Of the vast amount of qualities that fighters possess, or choose to develop, line familiarization is comparatively unimportant to most. With so much emphasis on speed, power, or limberness, it simply takes a back seat. However, as one increases his awareness as to just what *is* line familiarization, so too, will he allocate the amount of necessary time to develop it. When we use the word "line," we are actually saying *angle of attack*. The word "familiarization" is self-explanatory. Hence, line familiarization means to be familiar with the angle of attack that the opponent launches.

There is only one way to become familiar with anything. You must practice, or, as we say, put in the "flighttime." There are *no* free rides. A heavyweight professional boxer, for example, may spend fifteen years boxing...and get into an altercation with a white belt. Catching a front kick in the groin, he will *lose!* The boxer lost for one reason. He wasn't "familiar" with that *line* of attack.

Another scenario, perhaps more likely, would be that of a black belt of twenty years being used to sparring within the confines of his own style *only*, and being taken to the ground by a high school wrestler — and beaten. Obviously, no matter the style of the black belt, if he had incorporated the *lines* of attack *familiar* to the wrestler, he would have had, in theory, an appropriate counter.

Now we come to the catch-22: the word "theory." The aforementioned explanation of line familiarization is on the most rudimentary level. Now that we have a basic understanding, let's take it a step further and dissect the word *familiarization*. A JKD man strives to divorce the word "theory" from his arsenal. This, again, is done by implementing good old-fashioned flight-time. Therefore, to us that study JKD, familiarization does *not* consist of generically theorizing something, putting on paper the number of styles your art has incorporated — and *presto!!* — we have an armchair "eclectic" JKD man! To truly get familiar with the heat, you have to get into the kitchen.

The longer and more intensely one trains in different arenas, (i.e., boxers, wrestlers, Savatemen, Thai boxers, etc.) the more equipped one is to, as Bruce Lee put it, "Absorb what is useful, reject what is useless, and add what is specifically your own."

When this occurs, the attribute of line familiarization segues into one of the most important attributes one could ever possess, *awareness*. With awareness, we now can "intercept" and enter the path of becoming truly JKD!

CHAPTER VII
THE BROKEN BLUR

Speed

Before touching on the subject of speed in this book, we must understand that there are different kinds of speed. As simple as the word sounds, a JKD man does, or should, have a rather complex definition of the attribute that we are discussing. Speed is the ability to "close the crucial gap" between one's self and his opponents — with such economy, suddenness, or just raw explosiveness — and continue with a myriad of punches, elbows, knees, headbutts, etc. All of the aforementioned strikes are felt long before they are ever seen. This dynamic energy must escalate in intensity throughout the duration of blows (as opposed to dissipate, which is the norm).

As any physics major can tell you, weight times mass yields power and momentum. Weight times *speed* squares power and momentum. A piece of lead thrown at a person can well inflict pain. The same piece of lead hurled by a slingshot will inflict damage. The same piece of lead propelled by 240 grains of gunpowder will cause *instant* destruction. The only factor that differentiates pain from death is the speed at which the lead is propelled. Pause for a moment and visualize someone hitting you with an eighth of an ounce of lead...and then picture someone firing a .45 caliber at your head! With this image in mind, you can now have a more realistic idea about what we're really talking about.

To define speed as simply "miles per hour" would be akin to saying Mikhail Berishnikov is simply "coordinated." Once again, the multitude of reasons that we are blessed with a Berishnikov, or a Michael Jordan, or Sugar Ray Leonard, go far beyond the realm of a single word. Bruce's capacity to

Dan Inosanto and the author (left) working the *lop-sau* sensitivity drill.

overwhelm an opponent depended upon not only his speed, but the *quickness* in which his lightning-fast blows were delivered. To expound on this point further, these fast and quick blows must be delivered with impeccable "economy of motion." In other words, its not how fast you move, but how quick you get there.

I've enjoyed the privilege of training with fighters varying from Bill Wallace to more sublime artists such as Daniel Duby (the man who originally popularized Savate in America). Being exposed to Gung-Fu, Karate, Thai boxing, Kali, etc., has afforded me the opportunity to view "speed" from many different people's vantage points. To this day, the fastest man I've ever witnessed (who nearly set a world record in the 100-yard dash at 9.4) is Dan Inosanto. This is also the man who perhaps spent the most time witnessing the metamorphosis of Bruce's speed, on an almost daily basis. "Bruce just kept getting faster and faster," he says.

My point is twofold. Speed is not purely genetic. And speed is not just only a young man's game. Now that we have a clearer picture, let us examine some common denominators of people who possess an uncommon level of speed, at *any* age (i.e., John LaCoste, who, at age 85, could wield a Kali stick faster than we could see it).

All fast people have fast minds. A ceaseless bombardment of energy and lust for their chosen paths. To move fast, you must think fast. One must feel fast, the ability to convince one's brain that one is *unusually* fast.

A relaxation of the body must exist that dissipates antagonistic tension, which slows down our prime movers.

A "Gut feel" that inflicting damage is *not* synonymous with an "over-attempt" at delivering power (i.e., loose, snappy, sudden strikes as opposed to graphic, demonstrative motions).

The emphasis on retraction as opposed to thrusting. "If the strike goes out at fifty, it should come back at one hundred," Bruce Lee said.

Proper breathing. A relaxed, natural diaphragm with an emphasis on exhaling is most conducive for optimum speed.

Kinesthetic perception. This is the ability to "feel" one's muscles throughout a particular movement. As this process of "feeling" is cultivated, so also is the ability to recognize excess tension and make the proper neurological adjustments.

An unconventional, unindoctrinated mind. A mind that perceives the body's capabilities as unlimited as they really are. The body's biological age potential is 120 years; hence, middle-age is 60! The body doesn't have to slow down with age to nearly the degree (if any) that is commonly feared. However, be careful what you fear the most. It may come upon you.

I believe it would be helpful to go over the different points that I have cited. Allow yourself an open mind, and don't fool yourself if any particular point happens to "hit home." The major reason why most people take a defensive posture is because their "way" is violated. Allow me to conclude with the very crux in which all of Bruce Lee's principles flourished, and the very symbol of JKD: "When there is a way, man is bound," Bruce wrote. "There lies the limitations. A JKD man always strives to use no way as way, hence having no limitation for limitation."

Broken Rhythm

Rhythm is an attribute/quality no less important than speed, power, timing, etc. However, one can visualize qualities like speed by observing a cat, and power by watching Mike Tyson, making these concepts easier to grasp. Rhythm, on the other hand, is a bit more ambiguous. Where broken rhythm is presented, the concept becomes even more distorted. Webster's dictionary doesn't shed any further light for us either. Rhythm: Movement and fluctuations marked by the regular reoccurrence of related elements.

To put it simply, rhythm (as it applies to us) is the consistency between elements (plus movements) over time; the consistent lapse of time from one technique to the next, or the "in-between" time when no blows are exchanged. *Broken* rhythm changes this consistent pattern by the insertion of movements in between the "beats" of the established cadence. It can play an important role in a fighter's success. Development of broken rhythm can place in the following ways.

Learning. In order to break an opponent's rhythm, you must first learn to match his rhythm. Therefore, work drills in cadences of three (an odd number), with a pause in between sets (jab/catch-jab, catch-jab/catch, or punch-block-punch).

Memorize and master. Study and practice ways to change rhythms. Observe and develop the skills of the broken rhythm of boxers, fencers, and broken-rhythm martial art styles such as drunken monkey, etc. Apply these to your regular training routine.

Functionalize. When you spar, try to hit your opponent with half speed, then quarter speed, then double speed. See if you can hit your opponent in between his jab-cross rhythm combination.

Establish the rhythm, then break it in different ways. This will perplex your opponent first, and make it more difficult for him to respond effectively to your broken rhythm attacks. When a fighter uses the same rhythm, he establishes a "routine" which is a type of telegraphing. It leaves him more susceptible to his opponent's counters, stop-hits, and broken rhythms. He leaves himself open to be read, like so many pages in a book. When one cannot break the rhythm, he becomes "motorset," and/or "non-responsive."

To learn the patterns of fighting (and in many cases, life itself), and then *break* them, is to become free of conditioned routines and more responsive to your opponent (and world). Remember, Bruce said, "My technique is your technique, my movement is a result of your movement."

CHAPTER VIII
AWARENESS

Kinestetic Perception

Bruce Lee used to talk about the importance of "feeling" one's muscles throughout the range of a motion, or to perceive whether or not we are tense or loose. Once this is accomplished, we can then make the proper neurological adjustments. By adjustments, I mean that we can regulate the amount of tension on the desired muscle.

When we throw a punch or a kick, there are two types of muscles interacting simultaneously. The Prime Movers, and the Antagonistics. The Prime Movers are responsible for the desired motion, while the Antagonistics are the muscles on the other side of the joint that actually hinder that very movement (not unlike putting one's foot on the accelerator and the brake at one time). The degree of tension/contraction in the individual muscle, and the balance between the activities of different muscle groups, is what Bruce called "kinesthetic perception."

This perception is balanced by our central nervous system. As our kinesthetic perception improves, we not only learn to feel the state of our muscles, we can actually *change* that state. We can learn to reduce the tension of our Antagonistic muscles (letting off the brakes), while simultaneously increasing the intensity of our prime movers (stepping on the gas).

Let's pause for a moment and discuss how we can improve our kinesthetic perception. One way is to perform an isometric contraction. One is then forced to regulate the degree of tension on the muscle and joint. This provides us with a sort of barometer to gauge just how tense our muscles are, and the degree of contraction in those muscles. Therefore, in short, isometrics serve as a vehicle for both improving tendon strength and kinesthetic perception in the process.

Where to Stare

Anatomically speaking, the spot one chooses to look at on his opponent (during training, sparring, and fighting) can be very important. There are definite benefits in staring at certain areas over others. This is a controversial issue among different styles. Some arts will have you stare into "the window of the soul," the eyes. Certain arts believe that it is better to look at the forehead, between the eyes. Some say to look at the hips (the center of the person) because nothing moves before the hips. Other arts simply ignore the issue altogether... then the eyes of the student do what comes naturally, staring at the hands and feet. Let's discuss the various areas in more detail, and explore why Bruce Lee was not in favor of any of them.

First of all, staring into the eyes carries an air of mystery, and there is a myth that there is instant impotence the moment one looks into their opponent's eyes. The fact is, the eyes are not used to attack, and looking at them gives you no more information than staring at the ears.

Next, the hips. Unless your opponent is so tall that he literally towers above you, staring at the hips draws your attention too low, where vision is better below the point of focus than above. So, short of an opponent with hips close to eye level, the field of view is narrower the lower one looks, decreasing the peripheral vision.

The Elbow. In "the lab," this point of focus works fairly well, particularly in an art like Wing Chun. In "the field" (the street), however, the elbows of an opponent will be flopping around so much that it would be impossible to recognize or discern an attacking motion.

The arms and legs. Staring at the hands and feet is extremely unwise. Picture standing at the last six inches of a whip as it cracks. You get the point. The hands and feet are far too deceptive and quick. I fear that you'll end up feeling the strike before ever seeing it.

What should you look at? Bruce Lee felt that the chest offers the best signs of an opponent's attack. One should gaze into the chest without fixing the eyes. "You should know the color shirt your opponent is wearing, without reading the fine print," says

Dan Inosanto. The eyes pick up information by rapid movements (30-60 per second) called *scanning*. When the eye becomes heavily focused on a point, the process of scanning is restricted and the information is lost. The more specific the point of focus, the less information we receive. This "tunnel vision" suffocates the ability to respond to the many and varied possibilities that occur in combat. Staring at the chest area, without affixing your eyes, allows you to see the entire field of vision. It also allows you the best chance to know by which angle the opponent is attacking. The chest is the early-warning sign of a punch or a kick, and as you well know, we need early warning signs to be able to intercept.

The Peripheral Opponent

Regardless of the endeavor undertaken in life, *training*, as we have discussed, is the single most important aspect in developing one's fullest potential. In the martial arts, the more efficiently one trains, the more "intense" he becomes. Think about the intensity of other athletes' training required to reach their level of proficiency. Imagine sitting in on a Pittsburgh Steelers' practice during mid-season, or being ringside with Sugar Ray Leonard in training camp a few weeks before stepping into the ring with Marvin Hagler. Or perhaps watching Mikhail Barishnikov during a typical eight-hour practice day before a major performance. It's not likely that you are picturing these athletes having a tough time keeping their minds on training.

Imagine them now as martial artists. Would they drop what they are doing to answer the phone, or console a neighbor who's whining about the noise from a few rounds on the speed bag? It's doubtful. It's doubtful that any of these things would stop those athletes in the middle of a full-effort, roundhouse kicking session on the heavy bag.

These distractions are only a few that *do* affect many martial artists. I label these physical, or external, interruptions as the "Peripheral Opponent"; but this is only one side of the same coin. The other is within ourselves as we train. I call that the emotional (internal) Peripheral Opponent. It's that "little voice inside" that never shuts up. Are you going to get that raise at work? Will that big real estate deal come through? Where was the place that you stuck your lost keys yesterday?

Whether the distraction comes from within yourself, or from somebody else, the common denominator of virtually everyone who has attained an uncommon level of proficiency is victory over one of the toughest opponents, he Peripheral Opponent (PO).

Everyone has an exclusive PO, a monkey that most people don't even know is on their back. What could they accomplish if their monkey stayed in the zoo? Getting rid of the physical PO is much easier than exorcising the emotional PO. Physical distractions can be reduced by altering the *time* one trains (early morning or late afternoon) and *where* one trains (a private area without a phone). It should also be common knowledge to friends, relatives, wives, kids, and your family pet, that when you enter your "space" to train, you should *not* be disturbed! Be patient, however. It may take awhile to effectively train your circle of influence, but the effort will be most worthwhile to you over time.

Now we must contend with the toughest opponent of them all — you. Halfway through a great session on the heavy bag, that little voice in your head starts asking if you can make this month's house payment and still get the new tires that your car needs so much. You create an emotional opponent by even thinking about the way in which you are punching and kicking. To this kind of distraction Bruce Lee said, "Consciousness of the self is the greatest hindrance to mankind."

So, to put it succinctly, the martial artist who can cut off any internal dialogue is getting more out of one year of training than he would in ten years with his PO. This is because the information we get from the senses (stimulus) is "purely" interpreted by our brain and acted upon more efficiently by the firing of nerves in the correct muscles (response). Distractions radically decrease the entire stimulus/response process by giving a conflicting signal. This was one of Bruce's biggest revelations and had a lot to do with why, at an early age (early 30's), he attained such a high level. Bruce used to say, "I'm taking the elevator, while the others are still using the stairs."

It's 10:00 p.m. and you've been home for four hours (plenty of time to wind down from the day). You enter your training space, and now its "your time" (not Miller time). Lie on the ground, relaxing all parts of your body, eliminating internal dialogue. You will find that if you stop thinking, stop questioning, and stop listening to that little voice, you can begin training without your Peripheral Opponents. This is an advantage to you in emptying yourself to train as intensely as possible for the duration of the workout. This may take some practice to perfect, but worth the effort. It is sort of like waiting for the elevator, because once you catch it, its always faster than walking up those stairs.

CHAPTER IX
NOT-Kune-Do

Simply Eclectic

In the previous pages of this book, I have endeavored to define JKD, but that should not limit your interpretation of what it means. Just as so many men, for so many years, have given their subjective interpretations of Nostradamus and the Quatrains. Somehow this keeps us from taking for granted what certain people have accomplished.

My only objection lies where people take liberty with their opinions with absolutely no functional, practical background to reinforce them. This leads to my favorite phrase, "I've studied several different styles; therefore, like JKD, I'm eclectic!"

First and foremost, JKD is not eclectic. If you are studying several styles, please do not take this as a put-down. Eventually, common sense and a penchant for functionality would eventually lead you down that path. However, JKD is not eclectic. As Webster's dictionary simply puts it, *eclectic* means to pick and choose different systems or doctrines. Bruce didn't pick anything! He discovered common *flaws* and hacked away until the truth remained. If one truth lied within the realm of Thai boxing or Tai-Chi, he would simply note the common thread by way of noting a style that came closest to *his* "truth."

In my opinion, the worst thing ever discussed or written about JKD was/is how it is a conglomeration of arts, and thus eclectic. JKD is the synthesis of personal power (Bruce's power) by discovering the cause of *one's* own ignorance. However, JKD does have principles that one may interpret as rules or precursors. (For example, maintaining centerline; accommodating all four ranges; technique is second to attribute; an emphasis on movement as opposed to static stances; stop-hitting the opponent as opposed to blocking; etc.

None of the aforementioned characteristics detract from one's individualism. From that you then develop a more educated eye with which to separate functionalism from show — while simultaneously enhancing your ability to discover what aspect fits your individual needs. Your ignorance is not my ignorance, and the only way to distinguish our individual differences is to go through the process. To be eclectic, and randomly accumulate styles, simply puts us back in the role of clones. JKD is different for all of us. As Bruce put it,"Man himself is more important than any established style or system."

This is why Dan Inosanto always encouraged us, his students, to try other instructors in other styles. I used to wonder why I should seek out what had already been perfected by other men better than myself, namely, Bruce and Dan. Finally, I saw a most obvious point. Dan wanted us to discover the cause of *our own* ignorance. One can only do this by going through the process themselves. This is why the process is more important than the product.

No Room for Politics

The martial arts are a form of self-expression. Like any other art, if practiced intelligently and with diligence, its benefits will be integrated into our everyday life. By "intelligently," I mean practiced for the right reasons. I'm not speaking of how one uses his art, this is not a moral issue...I'm just speaking of the process. What is the goal? If one is in the art to achieve a particular rank, or in the art with the idea of becoming his instructor's "top student," that person is missing the boat. In fact, they haven't even located the water!

I see a growing trend to place certification over ability. This mentality is the breeding ground for politics, and politics are diametrically opposed to self-growth. I've said for many years that nothing speaks louder than action. One should let his

The author working with a small group of U.S. Navy SEALS in Virginia.

body do the talking, and worry less about the pecking order in the dojo — or a certificate on the wall. Pardon the cliche, but a person should strive to become the very best that they can be. The moment we become more concerned with the ornamentation, the certifications, the hierarchy, and so on, we compromise our original lust to simply become a great streetfighter. Isn't that what it's all about?

    Then we learn to control our mind, and, finally, our emotions. Where, in this formula, is there room for politics? This is why Bruce and Dan abandoned their JKD school in

The author (right) with Jeet Kune Do colleague Larry Hartsell.

Chinatown...so the students did not take the agenda as the truth, and the style as the "way."

Complacency

A subject I have always wished to address in a book is how to further improve one's skills in martial arts. Many martial artists assume that they've reached a stage of stagnation. In most cases, their intuition is correct. In ninety-nine percent of all endeavors in life, after a certain point, complacency sets in and growth ceases.

Martial arts are no different; in fact, they're *worse*. How many instructors have you heard brag that they've been studying their art for twenty years? I say that they have been studying it for four years — *and repeating it for sixteen*. In the average school that I see during a seminar, I invariably find the brown belts to be better fighters than the black belts. This is simply because the brown belts are still "hungry." Once one loses the lust that originally attracted them to the field that they have chosen, diminishing capacity sets in.

One reason for Bruce Lee's incredible ability was simply due to the fact that he *never* lost that lust to improve. To further complement that mentality, he despised the concept of having "belts." A black belt gives one a subconscious excuse to quit improving. One believes that he has finally "arrived." The *way* they have arrived is through that infamous black belt. This is why Bruce observed the philosophy of using "no way as way." "Once there is a way," he cited, "there lies the limitation."

Streetfighting . . . Not Even Comparable!!

We must first begin this discussion by defining just exactly what we mean be a streetfight. A JKD man's definition of a streetfight consists of but one rule: here are no rules! As we have said before, the linear logic of the Western mind loves to compare. Therefore, to define "which art is better," instead of first defining and clarifying the word "better," we would rather pit style A against style B, or fighter A against fighter B. The problem with this is that a streetfight is *too* multidimensional. For example, there aren't many street fighters, boxers, or martial artists whom I would give much of a chance if they were to fight Mike Tyson. There also aren't many streetfighters, etc., that I would give much of a chance fighting against Gene LeBell. Now, if we pit Tyson against LeBell, who would you put your money on? (I'd put mine on the promoter, outside of friends.)

I could very easily see both fighters entering the room, Tyson opening up with a jab followed by an overhand, and the fight lasting just a few seconds. On the other hand, I could just as easily see Tyson opening up with a jab, LeBell rushing him, closing the gap, and either choking him out, or body-slamming him into the next zip code. You see my point.

With *one* fight, the question of who is best becomes academic. Now let's insert one more person to the equation, Larry Hartsell. Larry doesn't quite have the size of LeBell, or the punching power of Tyson, but he has been trained extensively in trapping, in which knees, elbows, and head-butts are very prevalent. Basically, to beat Larry, you'd have to kill him! Now oblige me for just one minute.

Mike Tyson vs. Larry Hartsell. Tyson opens up with his jab, Hartsell follows with a vicious thigh kick, followed by a straight blast with a succession of elbows and knees. The winner...Hartsell!

Hartsell vs. LeBell. Hartsell opens up with a kick, LeBell grabs the leg and takes Larry to the ground. Now, in his game, he easily chokes Larry out. Winner...Gene LeBell.

Our final fight pits *LeBell against Tyson.* LeBell opens up with a double-leg take-down. Tyson stop-hits with a jab, followed by a flurry of punches. The winner...Tyson.

Well, now we have a problem. Fighter A beats fighter B, fighter B beats fighter C, and fighter C beats fighter A. There goes our linear logic. It now becomes quite obvious that one cannot say with authority that one person can beat another person in *a* fight. Like in professional football, any given team can be victorious on any given day. That's why most professional sports have a *series* of games. Perhaps we could be more accurate in evaluating a streetfighter if we had a series of fights. Say, best out of 10.

The purpose of this short lesson is to show the readers that streetfighting is a bit more complex than would first appear. Before we compare fighter "A" to fighter "B," remember that there is always fighter "C" around the block!

CHAPTER X
A PARTING SHOT

Well, where do we go from here? You've just finished reading a compilation of the knowledge that has taken me 20 years to obtain. I have condensed my information so as to be as economical as possible for you. And, it is important to me that you have a road map throughout your training in JKD. Remember one thing. Keep striving to be your best, never be limited in your quest for further knowlege, always allow room to accept new concepts and ideas in the martial arts. In other words, keep yourself as an empty cup, always prepared to be filled.

A typical seminar tour: Paul with some of his instructors in Manhattan in 1984.

PART THREE:
APPLICATIONS

1) Paul (left) squares off with the opponent, continually moving. 2) Paul fakes high. (In JKD, when a fake precedes a strike, it is usually a Progressive Indirect Attack.) 3) He now executes a thigh kick from Thai boxing. 4) Moving in, he finishes with an inside foot sweep (several arts use this move).

1-1

1-2

1-3

1-4

1) Paul (right) squares off with the opponent. 2) He fakes high to draw the attention on the face. 3) He now enters with a low kick to the inner shin. 4) He now traps the opponent's front hand (the trap is taken from Wing Chun). 5) Paul moves in and 6) executes a knee which is borrowed from Thai boxing.

2-1

2-2

2-3

2-4

JEET KUNE DO: Its Concepts and Philosophies • 59

2-5

2-6

1) Paul (right) initiates with a *jeet-tek* (a sort of side kick used more, however, to stop-hit) and 2) moves into a *pak-sao* from Wing Chun. The opponent blocks with the rear hand. 3) Paul traps the rear hand and executes a palm strike, lifting the chin. 4) He ends the altercation with a horizontal elbow across the Adam's apple.

3-1

3-2

3-3

3-4

1) Paul (right) squares off with the opponent. 2) He fakes low to draw the attention down. 3) He now enters with a jab from boxing and 4) follows with the beginning of a series of straight punches from Wing Chun. 5) A continuation of straight punches (commonly called the "Wing Chun straight blast" or *jik-chun-choy*. 6) Paul finishes with the tip of the elbow raking across the temple.

4-1

4-2

JEET KUNE DO: Its Concepts and Philosophies • 63

4-3

4-4

64 • JEET KUNE DO: Its Concepts and Philosophies

4-5

4-6

JEET KUNE DO: Its Concepts and Philosophies • 65

1) Paul (right) squares off with the opponent. 2) He fakes high, drawing the attention up. 3) He now enters with a palm strike to the groin and 4) follows up with an elbow strike.

5-1

5-2

5-3

5-4

1) Paul (left) squares off with the opponent, 2) who throws the typical side kick. 3) Paul slips back and simultaneously kicks the opponent's groin. 4) He now enters with a trap, jabbing the eyes. 5) He follows up with a vertical elbow. 6) He grabs the hair and positions for a forearm strike. 7) Paul finishes with a horizontal elbow to the throat.

6-1

6-2

6-3

6-4

JEET KUNE DO: Its Concepts and Philosophies • 69

6-5

6-6

6-7

1) Paul (right) squares off with the opponent. 2) The opponent attempts a low roundhouse kick and Paul uses a front knee to destroy the kick (a technique from Kali) and as an entry. 3) He enters with a *pak-sao* trap (from Wing Chun). 4) Paul re-traps the arm and 5) finishes up with a punch.

7-1

7-2

7-3

7-4

7-5

1) Paul (left) squares off with the opponent, **2)** who side kicks to the midsection. **3)** Paul uses a front elbow to destroy the kick (from Kali) and as an entry. **4)** He now traps the opponent and **5)** finishes with a knee to the thigh.

8-1

8-2

8-3

8-4

8-5

1) Paul (left) squares off with the opponent, 2) who throws a low side kick. 3) Paul simply raises his knee, 4) traps the front hand, and 5) finishes with an elbow to the temple.

9-1

9-2

9-3

9-4

9-5

1) Paul (right) squares off with the opponent, 2) who throws a low roundhouse to the thigh. 3) Paul destroys the shin with a knee and 4) enters with a blast.

10-1

10-2

10-3

10-4

82 • JEET KUNE DO: Its Concepts and Philosophies

1) Paul (left) squares off with the opponent, 2) who executes a high round kick. 3) Paul uses his front elbow to destroy the kick, 4) then smashes the opponent's shin, and 5) follows up with a shot to the groin.

11-1

11-2

11-3

11-4

11-5

1) Paul (left) squares off with the opponent, 2) who delivers a jab. 3) Paul zones away from the rear hand and executes an eye jab, 4 & 5) followed by a Savate kick. 6 & 7) He finishes with an elbow from Thai boxing.

12-1

12-2

12-3

12-4

12-5

12-6

12-7

1) Paul (left) squares off with the opponent, **2)** who jabs. **3)** Paul jabs the eyes from the inside line and then **4 & 5)** simultaneously punches and delivers a groin kick.

13-1

13-2

13-3

13-4

JEET KUNE DO: Its Concepts and Philosophies • 91

13-5

1) Paul (right) squares off with the opponent. 2) The opponent jabs and Paul destroys the nerve on the inside of the arm (a move from Kali). 3) He jabs the eyes with the rear hand and 4) enters with a back fist. 5) The opponent blocks with the rear hand, which Paul grabs, using a *lop-sao*. 6) He then breaks the elbow, 7) lowers his elevation to deliver a groin slap, and 8) rises up to a head butt. The complete sequence should take approximately two seconds.

14-1

14-2

14-3

14-4

94 • JEET KUNE DO: Its Concepts and Philosophies

14-5

14-6

JEET KUNE DO: Its Concepts and Philosophies • 95

14-7

14-8

1) Paul (right) squares off with the opponent, 2) who jabs. 3) Paul destroys the jab using his elbow and 4) continues the motion into the eyes. 5) Paul re-traps using a Wing Chun *gum-sao*, and 6) finishes with a straight punch.

15-1

15-2

15-3

15-4

15-5

15-6

1) Paul (right) squares off with the opponent, 2) who attempts a spinning back kick. 3) Paul raises his knee and 4) intercepts the spin with a kick to the small of the back.

16-1

16-2

16-3

16-4

1) Paul (left) squares off with the opponent, 2) who delivers a low fake. 3) Paul raises to an ear slap, which the opponent blocks. 4) Paul traps both hands, 5) moves forward to a mid-point, and 6) continues to the opponent's rear and executes a choke.

17-1

17-2

17-3

17-4

17-5

17-6

104 • JEET KUNE DO: Its Concepts and Philosophies

1) Paul (left) squares off with the opponent. 2) Paul jabs and the opponent blocks with the front hand. 3) Paul moves in and wrenches the elbow, and 4) finishes with a knee.

18-1

18-2

JEET KUNE DO: Its Concepts and Philosophies

18-3

18-4

1) Paul (right) starts with a reference point. 2) He enters with a Wing Chun *pak-sao*, which the opponent blocks. 3) Paul traps his rear hand and spins the opponent's head. 4) He continues the spin and 5) finishes by grabbing the head and executing a neck break.

19-1

19-2

19-3

19-4

108 • JEET KUNE DO: Its Concepts and Philosophies

19-5

1) Paul (right) starts with a low reference point. 2) He enters with a back fist, which the opponent blocks. 3) Paul zones out and punches low, 4) cocks his fist at midpoint, and 5) traps the opponent's hand. 6) He finishes with an elbow.

20-1

20-2

20-3

20-4

20-5

20-6

1) Paul (right) starts from a reference point. 2) He enters with a Wing Chun *pak-sao*. 3) The opponent crosses the center line and Paul *lop-saos*. 4) He continues the *lop-sao*, 5) grabs the opponent's neck and pulls in his head. 6) Paul moves to a mid-point and 7) smashes the opponent's head with the inner elbow. 8) He pulls him back into a head butt, and 9) finishes with a knee to the temple.

21-1

21-2

21-3

21-4

21-5

21-6

21-7

21-8

116 • JEET KUNE DO: Its Concepts and Philosophies

1-3) Paul (right) and his partner executing an energy drill called *chi-sao*.

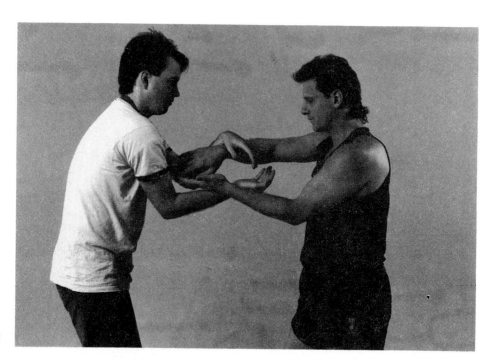

22-1

22-2

22-3

1-5) Paul (right) and his partner, starting from a Thai boxing position, practice different variables, i.e., elbows, knees and head butts.

23-1

23-2

23-3

23-4

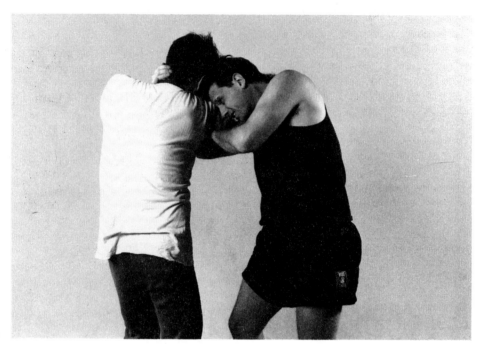

23-5

ABOUT THE AUTHOR

Paul Vunak is one of a handful of full-instructors worldwide in the art of Jeet Kune Do, under Dan Inosanto. Mr. Vunak is the exclusive hand-to-hand combat instructor for the Navy Special Forces Unit (the Navy SEALS). Paul also is one of the few Savate intructors in the United States and has black belts in Kenpo Karate and Tae Kwon Do. His company, "Progressive Fighting Systems," maintains a staff of instructors worldwide, promulgating the instruction of Jeet Kune Do and perpetuating the teaching of Bruce Lee's art.